African Magic Series

THE ORISHAS

MONIQUE JOINER SIEDLAK

Oshun
Publications

The Orishas© Copyright 2020 by Monique Joiner Siedlak

ISBN: 978-1-950378-69-2

All rights reserved.

The content contained within this book may not be reproduced, duplicated or transmitted without direct written permission from the author or the publisher.

Under no circumstances will any blame or legal responsibility be held against the publisher, or author, for any damages, reparation, or monetary loss due to the information contained within this book, either directly or indirectly.

Legal Notice:

This book is copyright protected. It is only for personal use. You cannot amend, distribute, sell, use, quote or paraphrase any part, or the content within this book, without the consent of the author or publisher.

Disclaimer Notice:

Please note the information contained within this document is for educational and entertainment purposes only. All effort has been executed to present accurate, up to date, reliable, complete information. No warranties of any kind are declared or implied. Readers acknowledge that the author is not engaged in the rendering of legal, financial, medical or professional advice. The content within this book has been derived from various sources. Please consult a licensed professional before attempting any techniques outlined in this book.

By reading this document, the reader agrees that under no circumstances is the author responsible for any losses, direct or indirect, that are incurred as a result of the use of the information contained within this document, including, but not limited to, errors, omissions, or inaccuracies.

Cover Design by MJS

Cover Image by FairytaleDesign@depositphotos.com

Published by Oshun Publications

www.oshunpublications.com

Books in Series
_____

African Spirituality Beliefs and Practices
Hoodoo
Seven African Powers: The Orishas
Cooking for the Orishas
Lucumi: The Ways of Santeria
Voodoo of Louisiana
Haitian Vodou
Orishas of Trinidad
Connecting with your Ancestors

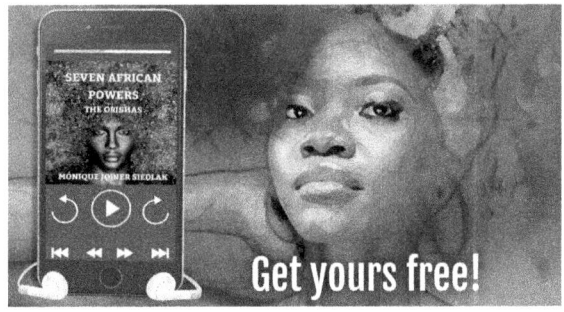

Want to learn about African Magic, Wicca, or even Reiki while cleaning your home, exercising, or driving to work? I know it's tough these days to simply find the time to relax and curl up with a good book. This is why I'm delighted to share that I have books available in audiobook format.

Best of all, you can get the audiobook version of this book or any other book by me for free as part of a 30-day Audible trial.

Members get free audiobooks every month and exclusive discounts. It's an excellent way to explore and determine if audiobook learning works for you.

If you're not satisfied, you can cancel anytime within the trial period. You won't be charged, and you can still keep your book. To choose your free audiobook, visit:

www.mojosiedlak.com/audiobooks

Want To Be First To Know?!

Contents

Introduction — xi

1. Father Figure of the Orishas — 1
2. Lord of the Crossroads — 3
3. The Orisha of Iron — 5
4. The Mother Spirit — 9
5. The Orisha of Love — 11
6. The King of the Religion — 15
7. Queen of the Cemetery — 19

Conclusion — 23
References — 25
About the Author — 27
More Books by Monique Joiner Siedlak — 29
Last Chance to Sign Up — 31

Introduction

Orishas are deities who make up part of the native spirituality of the Yoruba people. This ethnic group consists of 40 million individuals in all, who can be found living in southern and central Benin and Nigeria.

Though an Orisha is interpreted as a deity in this religion, they are not just perceived as divine entities. The belief is that an Orisha comes to be when a supernatural power commands it to be, an ancestor idealizes it, or it is associated with a natural item.

It is a multidimensional unity that joins both forces, people, and objects to utilize and take in the different spirits' rewards.

In the Yoruba custom, there are reported to be anything from 400 to 1,440 different Orisha. Followers believe that day-to-day life's capacity relies on the correct insight and behavior associated with their "Ori." In actual terms, Ori means head, and in terms of spirituality, it relates to the soul and one's future.

Devotees also maintain that by carrying out rituals and honoring the Orishas, they will reach their destinies, which God had designed for them before their birth.

Introduction

The relationship between Orishas and humans is a mutual one. Orishas require devotion and worship by human beings to continue to exist in the world and spirit realms.

J. Omosade Awolalu, a Nigerian scholar, separated the Orishas into three categories: the primordial divinities, deified ancestors, and natural forces.

Primordial divinities are deities or beings that existed before the birth of the world. Some existed before the arrival of humankind. They emanated straight from God and with no human interference. They are also known as "Aro Orun," people of Heaven. Some Orishas are also known as "Irunmole," the world's first inhabitants, who are now considered sacred beings who still reside both in and on Earth.

Deified ancestors are the individuals who lived on the Earth after it was molded. These people had such a remarkable impact on the planet that their descendants thus continued to cherish and share in their memory. These people who shaped the world were warriors, queens, kings, cultural heroes, and heroines who greatly influenced the Yoruba community and are still celebrated today.

Lastly, there are the natural forces. From the Yoruba perspective, this is an element of the world that has many benefits for both the spirit and humans. Spirits may reside in the earth, mountains, rivers, trees, lakes, and the wind. Worshippers gather at sacred locations where their adoration and devotions are directed at the spirit which resides in these natural phenomena.

In the 18th and 19th centuries, when individuals from these countries were enslaved and sent to the Americas, they took their practices and beliefs. Because of this, the legs of this religion still exist in parts of South America and the Caribbean.

Regardless of the impact that other mainstream religions have made on cultural beliefs and practices, the Yoruba people still look to the deities when needing help, advice, or support.

Let us take a look at seven of the most profound Orishas.

ONE

Father Figure of the Orishas

Obatala is known to be a wise Orisha and is often also known as the chief and judge. He is married to Yemeya, who is the mother figure of all Orishas and is the Goddess of the Oceans. According to some patakis, Obatala is the father of all human beings. He and Yemeya created a lot of children. One day he got very drunk when making humans because he was thirsty and he drank some palm wine. Under the influence of the wine, he made some deformed humans. After he sobered up, he realized what he had done. He swore from that day that he would never drink and now every handicapped or deformed person has a special place in his heart. He takes extra care of them. Obatala shows mercy and compassion because of the fact that he realizes that he erred once when he got drunk on the palm wine. This is why he is also known to be the fairest Orisha of all.

Very Strong

Obatala was a very strong warrior when he was young and saw many injustices and wrongs being committed during those wars. Which is why when he became an Orisha, he vouched for peace. His experience on the battlefields angered him and now, as a judge, he is very much involved in the law and issues of justice. He will be involved in any kind of legal case or court issue. You can invoke him during such times for his help. However, do not invoke him if you are guilty unless you are willing to be punished for it. Obatala is also involved in karmic justice. If you think someone has done a karmic injustice to you, you can call to him for help. He will help you and make you be strong. He encourages humans to take responsibility for their irrational actions.

Obatala has no gender and is thought to be asexual. This signifies why he is rightfully thought to be the father of human beings. He has no patience for the gender fights which break out in the human community.

All in White

Obatala is also associated with the color white. He is known as the God of white clothing and even loves his food to be white in color. He loves white offerings with no spices or even alcohol. People tend to spread a white cotton ball on the offerings they make to Obatala to please him. People can even offer him eggs, rice, mushrooms, water, milk, crushed egg shells, snail shells, myrrh or tobacco. Obatala worshippers dance in white costumes and offer white pumpkin, coconut milk and light up sandalwood incense to please this Orisha.

Obatala is often found in churches, libraries, universities, mountains, forest and the military. His number is 8 and his feast day is the 24th of September. His tool is a horsetail fly whisk. All of the animals sacrificed to Obatala should be white in color such as she-goats, guinea hens, doves, and hens.

TWO

Lord of the Crossroads

Elegba, also known as Legba or Elewa, Elleguá, Elegua is one of the most important Orishas to exist. He is known to be the first orisha to be created by Olodumare herself. He is known to be the Lord of the Crossroads because without him, our prayers to the other Orishas would never reach. He represents the beginning and end of life as well as the opening and closing paths of life. Which is why when people worship or make offerings to the other Orishas; they make sure to make an offering to Elegba as well to have his blessing. He facilitates divination by communicating to the other orishas for us. Otherwise the doors of communication with the other orishas would remain closed.

Fun and Games

Elegba is also very commonly known as the trickster, troublemaker or even experimenter. This is because he likes to test humanity. He is a witness to everything a man says or does and he tests our word, the truth and integrity of it. This is why people know him as a trickster. During the reception of the Warriors in initiation, Elegba is the first orisha to be received before Oshun, Ochosi and Ogun. He can speak for all of the other Orishas which is why people tend to make him an offering first before the others. He is recognized as the most crucial and important Orisha during such ceremonies.

Different Appearances

Elegba is often represented as a child and sometimes an old man. He is represented as a child because he is known to like child-like things such as toy soldiers, balls, whistles and even candies. Apart from the childish things, he likes silver coins and is often depicted as wearing a straw hat or a red kerchief. Elegba's colors are mainly red and black. His lucky number is 3 and any multiple of 3. His day of the week is Monday and the 3rd day of each month. In Cuba, Elegba has saint days on 6th of January and 13th of June. On these days, the people of Cuba throw a huge feast to honor this orisha.

Apart from candy, this orisha is also known to like toasted corn, strong alcohol, rum, vino seco, cigars, smoked hutia meat, smoked fish and red palm oil. These foods make a great offering for him and people often tend to offer these foods to the orisha on Mondays. Elegba is also the most sexual entity. His statue is often represented as him having an erect penis.

Elegba, Eshu and The Pomba Gira are thought to be separate entities but are closely related. Many people like to think of the 3 of them as siblings. Elegba is thought to be the most important out of all three which why he is made an offering first. The rest of the two follow after Elegba. All the world's doorways, whether physical or emotional, are controlled by them. They can make a person the luckiest in the world or they can make a person the most unlucky person on earth. It all depends on them.

THREE

The Orisha of Iron

Ogun is known to be a very powerful warrior who has creativity and intelligence when it comes to making new tools. He protects his people from injustice. He is known as the father of civilization because if it were not for his creative tools, the earth would be full of the wilderness. If it were not for his strength, the path from heaven to earth would never have been cleared for the Orishas and humanity to thrive on earth. Ogun's tools were the tools which helped create new buildings and cities.

His Two Sides

Ogun has a protective nature, like a loving and overprotective father. He can be the fiercest and angriest bloodthirsty warrior whose tools thirst for the blood of his enemies. However, he can also be the Orisha who helps removes cancers from humans and forges new innovative tools. Ogun is very loyal and is often found in densely forested areas where he likes to hunt with his best-hunting partners, Elegua and Ochosi. These three signifies one of the Orishas to be received during the reception of the Warriors initiation. Ogun's shrine is an iron cauldron which is filled with iron tools and supplements.

Ogun Makes the Sacrifice

Ogun is the one who invented the knife. However, he does not own it. It is Obatala who owns it. Ogun was just asked to make the knife for him. It is with Ogun's strong and piercing energy that animals are sacrificed. This way, it is not the orisha who takes the animal's life, it is Ogun. This is often reflected in the phrase which people recite before sacrificing an animal: "Ogun shoro shoro, eyebale kuwo".

Emerging as the Orisha of Iron

There is a Pataki related to Ogun which tells how he became the Orisha of iron. The Orishas and humans were once living on the land created by Obatala. Orishas and the humans alike leveled the land and cleared the trees from the land so that they could cultivate on it. However, the problem arose when, as the population began to increase, they needed more land for the people to live and build houses on. Their tools, however, were not enough. They were made of wood, stone or soft metal. So, all the Orishas met and decided to clear the land with their tools one by one. All except Olokun disagreed, saying that she had nothing to do with the land and that her domain was the oceans and seas. Osanyin, Orisha of medicine, decided to clear the field first. However, his bush knife was made of soft metal and it became bent. The same happened with Oko and Eshu. Seeing the Orishas fail, Ogun with his iron knife set out and cleared the land and fields. He came back showing his undamaged knife. He declined to give the secret of iron to the other Orishas. The Orishas offered to make him their ruler for which he agreed and gave them the knowledge of iron. However one day he was cast out because he looked messy, muddy and bloody. The Orishas rejected him but the people, to this day, still remember and worship him.

FOUR

The Mother Spirit

Yemeya is often also spelled as Yemoja, Yemanja, Lemanja or even Yemalla. Yemeya literally means "Mother of Water". Even though she is the Goddess of the vast and open oceans seas, she is also worshipped near lakes, wells or lagoons. Anywhere there is water; Yemeya is likely to be present. In West Africa, they worship Yemeya as a river deity but in Brazil and Cuba, they worship her only as a sea/ocean Goddess. This mother spirit has a soft place in her heart for all the women of the world, especially pregnant women. It takes a lot to anger this Goddess because she doesn't get easily riled up. But when she does, you should expect a huge hurricane your way. She is very loving, but she is very powerful.

Motherhood's Greatest

Yemeya loves her children and cares a lot for them. Their sorrow is almost as if it is Yemeya's sorrows. She protects women especially and cures infertility for women who cannot conceive a child. She is almost always involved during childbirth, child care, parenting, healing, love, and conception.

Yemeya is also often depicted as a mermaid with 2 tails who is associated with the moon, water, and feminine mysteries. According to a Yoruba Pataki, when Yemeya's waters broke, it caused such a great flood that the water bodies on earth were created and that she gave birth to many human beings from her womb. In some cultures, Yemeya is also known to have given birth to the sun, moon, stars and many Orishas. She will unleash her wrath upon anyone who threatens her children.

According to Yoruba patakis and myths, when the slaves were transported across the oceans, it was Yemeya who protected and nurtured them. It was Yemeya who looked after them. She is the wife of Obatala, the chief, and judge. Yemeya also often gets depressed over her children. However, she is a stylish Goddess and despises gaudy things. Which is why in Brazil, the worshippers throw a huge feast for this Goddess. On 2nd February, everyone dresses up in white and goes down to the ocean to send her gifts and offerings on boats.

Giving Her Gifts

Yemeya's offerings should be laid out in a stylish setting. Seafood on a gold or silver plate, a fruit basket, and some excellent white wine are known to be the best way to please this stylish Goddess. What pleases her, even more, is if you donate to a family or children's charity or help a single mom. Yemeya also loves foamy lattes.

Apart from the oceans and large water bodies, Yemeya can be found in weddings, maternity wards or daycare centers.

Yemeya is known to wear a dress with seven skirts that represent the seven seas. With her favorite colors being blue and white and her favorite animals are the peacocks and ducks. Her number is 7, to signify the seven seas. The tools of Yemeya are the boat steering wheel, oars, anchors, and machetes. Cowrie shells are known to represent her wealth.

FIVE

The Orisha of Love

Oshun is rightly known as the Orisha of love because she was the last Orisha to be born out of the love Olodumare had for creations. Many people compare Oshun to the Greek God Aphrodite. This is because Oshun is not only the Orisha of Love but also femininity, beauty and sensuality. Oshun is known to usually live near rivers.

Loved By Women

Oshun is very popularly worshipped in Africa especially by women. This is because she represents each and every phase of a woman's life. Often times, she is depicted as a woman of mixed race with long locks of hair carrying a fan and a mirror. This depicts her beauty. Oshun is also known to be a powerful sorceress. Some say that she intoxicates her lovers by weaving different spells to trap them in. Oshun loves Aña drums. Whenever she feels sorrowful, she dances to forget her worries. Oshun is a very loving and protective Orisha but she is also known to turn cruel and furious against those who disrespect her or her children. Forgiveness by this Orisha is very hard to expect. It is also said that whenever Oshun possesses her olorishas, if they appear crying then it is a good sign. Crying means that the tears are tears of joy. If the olorishas appear laughing, it is a bad sign. The laughing is maniacal laughing which represents her anger.

Children of Oshun

Oshun is also popularly known as the mother of the Ibeji, the twin orishas, which were fathered by Chango. She was accused of being a witch for mothering the twins after which she kicked out the Ibeji twins. The twins were then adopted by Oya (some say that they were adopted by Yemeya). Oshun was then destitute and cursed. However she was soon blessed by another child by Olofi which was named Ideu.

There is also a Pataki related to Oshun and Iroko. Oshun was once preparing for a party. She dressed herself up in gold, jewelry and perfumes and passed by a small village where some small children were playing. She was happy when she saw them and sprinkled honey on them after which they bowed to her. Oshun sat down near Iroko, a Cieba Tree, when a tear dropped. Iroko asked Oshun what was wrong to which she replied that she missed having children and wanted Iroko to help her bear children. Iroko agreed to the price that Oshun must accompany Iroko every now and then to which she agreed.

Oshun bore a son and Iroko, hearing about the good news, asked Oshun. Oshun only replied that yes she had borne a son and kept walking, forgetting her promise. Every now and then she would promise Iroko that she would bring a goat or bring her son to meet him. One day, Ideu sat under Iroko and told him that he was the son of Oshun. Becoming happy, he brought Ideu to his domain to tell him stories. Years passed and Oshun could not find her son. Iroko saw how depressed Oshun was and soon brought Ideu back to Oshun. After which, Oshun's children were never allowed to meet Iroko.

SIX

The King of the Religion

Also spelled and pronounced as Shango, Chango is a very important Orisha in Santeria. He is one of the four pillars in Santeria and every person has to receive him during initiation whether or not they are his children. Apart from being the King of the religion on earth, Chango is also the Orisha for male virility, leadership, thunder, fire, drumming, and dancing.

A Strong King He Was Not

Chango is known to not be as effective as a king should be when he was alive. However, after his death, he worked miracles for the other Orishas. Chango is also known to have had many female lovers and was an exquisite dancer and drummer. Chango also has a magical and powerful mortar which allows him to spit fire from his mouth. A double-headed ax is his favorite weapon and his residence is at the top of the royal palm tree.

His Relationship

There is a popular Pataki related to Chango and Oya. Chango was once at a party, drinking and dancing and having the time of his life. He was enjoying so much that he did not realize that some of his enemies were outside the party watching him. As soon as the party died down and all the guests left, Chango staggered to a corner where an enemy was waiting for him. The enemy quickly trapped him and locked him in a small cell. Chango and Oya had had a fling.

Chango's Rescue

He had kept his pilon and mortar at her house. Days passed and Oya grew worried because Chango did not show up. Oya wondered about his pilon and mortar. She saw that the inside the mortar was gleaming and a clear liquid formed. Seeing that Chango had been trapped in a cell, Oya became furious. At that moment, she called upon lightning to help her rescue him. Kissing the liquid in the mortar and soon her lips and mouth burned. No water could ease the burning and fire spat out. The lightning came and took her to Chango. As she reached there, Oya screamed a war cry and a burst of fire erupted from her mouth.

Chango's enemies soon scattered and Oya released Chango. She told him about how she rescued him as he could not remember. It upset Chango that Oya pried in his mortar but was grateful. Ever since Oya now accompanies Chango in fights and wars.

Children of Chango

Chango fathered the Ibeji twins as well as Boromu and Borosia, the children born because of Yeggua's rape. Many Orishas used to complain about Chango's unruly and egoistic attitude. However, through many trials and errors and a reality check from Obatala, Chango soon matured and learned gracefulness and charm. This Orisha teaches us that no matter how many mistakes we make, we can always turn around and redeem ourselves. He is very loving and compassionate towards his children and all Orishas.

Corresponding to Chango

His colors are red, white and gold. His numbers are 4 or 6 or both. Spicy foods, alcohol, chili peppers, tobacco, okra, and cornbread make great offerings for this Orisha.

SEVEN

Queen of the Cemetery

A female warrior, Oya is a very strong and powerful warrior. She is the owner of the marketplace and guards the door of the cemetery. Being a warrior, she rides into battle while wielding lightning and her machetes. She is often accompanied to battle by her favorite lover, Chango. Oya can raise the army of the dead during a fight or a battle and patakis often say that Oya has been known to use tornados as a weapon as well. Many patakis say that Oya is literally a tornado.

Strong and Strict Love

Oya is like a compassionate but strict mother. She is known to give her children and worshippers some time to cry and whine about their problems and get it all off of their chests. However, she expects you to pull it together. She will guide you along the path and help you with the difficulties and challenges you face. However she will not do the literal work for you as she expects you yourself to do it. Oya is also known to be a witch. She is comfortable around occult objects and is said to have strong connections with the ancestors. Which is why she should be involved in any and every ancestral ceremonies.

Oya guards the graveyards. It is her main duty to keep away the grave robbers and disrespectors of the ancestors. She will hunt them down mercilessly and punish them for it.

Separated From Her Husband

Oya is known to be the third wife of Chango. Chango chose Oya to be his wife after his first wife, Oba, and second wife, Oshun, had a feud and big rivalry between them which blew up into a war. Chango, after that incident, wanted a much more balanced and supportive woman. According to some patakis, Oya and Chango never lived together. Oya loved her peace and liked living in the forests. Whereas Chango, who was already tired of rivalries between women, was a busy man. Both of them gave each other space however they loved each other fiercely. Till they died, they always stayed connected.

People often tend to find lessons in these patakis and stories of Oya and Chango. The most common lesson is that when people are young, they find familial duty and sexual attraction to be the most important aspects. Which is why Chango first wife was a dutiful woman and his second wife was very visually stunning. However, with time and age, once we have settled and become well established, all we look for is pleasure and peace. Our priorities change, just like Chango's when he chose Oya to be his wife. So, a woman who wants to be her husband's everything should learn to balance Chango's three wives: Oba, Oshun and Oya.

There are different views on the way Oya looks. Some say that she is so incredibly beautiful that she has to wear a veil to hide her beauty from men. Some say that she wears a veil because she has a scarred, burnt and horrendous face which, if anyone looked at, would die.

Oya enjoys dark colored and sweet foods as her offering.

Conclusion

These concepts, practices, and traditions have continued through the test of time. They have been modified and sculpted by individuals from across the world, including those from America, Brazil, Cuba, and Haiti, and have been integrated with other doctrines such as Catholicism.

The following is important because it has endured for hundreds of years in other countries, distantly from its roots in Africa. Still, so much has changed since then, the religion nevertheless remains intact.

In Haiti, the Yoruba people's beliefs, blended with the Fon, serve as Voodoo's base foundation. Cubans call the beliefs Lucumi, which is "friend" in the Yoruba language. Religions and beliefs have also migrated as far as Brazil, where it is recognized as Candomble or Macumba. It has even found new roots in Los Angeles, identified as Santeria, or "worship of saints" in Spanish.

Though there are many colorful Orishas, the Yoruba still affiliate themselves with one supreme being or God who created the universe. It was the Orisha whom God assigned to watch after the Earth and its citizens.

References

Brandon, G. (n.d.). Oshun. Encyclopedia Britannica. https://www.britannica.com/topic/Oshun

Changó. (n.d.). About Santeria. https://www.aboutsanteria.com/changoacute.html

Eleguá/Eshu. (n.d.). About Santeria. https://www.aboutsanteria.com/eleguaacuteeshu.html

Eshu. (n.d.). Encyclopedia Britannica. https://www.britannica.com/topic/Eshu

Mitchell, R. (1988, February 7). Power of the Orishas: Santeria, an ancient religion from Nigeria, is making its presence felt in Los Angeles. Los Angeles Times. https://www.latimes.com/archives/la-xpm-1988-02-07-tm-40762-story.html

Obatalá, Owner of All Heads. (n.d.). About Santeria. https://www.aboutsanteria.com/obatalaacute.html

Ochún. (n.d.). About Santeria. https://www.aboutsanteria.com/ochuacuten.html

Ogun. (2002, September 24). Wikipedia, the free encyclopedia. https://en.wikipedia.org/wiki/Ogun

References

Ogun. (n.d.). About Santeria. https://www.aboutsanteria.com/oguacuten.html

Oshun. (n.d.). Encyclopedia Britannica. https://www.britannica.com/topic/Oshun

Oyá. (n.d.). About Santeria. https://www.aboutsanteria.com/oyaacute.html

Santeria deities. (n.d.). BBC - Home. https://www.bbc.co.uk/religion/religions/santeria/beliefs/orishas.shtml

Yemayá. (n.d.). About Santeria. https://www.aboutsanteria.com/yemayaacute.html

Yemoja. (2002, October 4). Wikipedia, the free encyclopedia. https://en.wikipedia.org/wiki/Yem%E1%BB%8Dja

About the Author

Monique Joiner Siedlak is a writer, witch, and warrior on a mission to awaken people to their greatest potential through the power of storytelling infused with mysticism, modern paganism, and new age spirituality. At the young age of 12, she began rigorously studying the fascinating philosophy of Wicca. By the time she was 20, she was self-initiated into the craft, and hasn't looked back ever since. To this day, she has authored over 40 books pertaining to the magick and mysteries of life.

To find out more about Monique Joiner Siedlak artistically, spiritually, and personally, feel free to visit her **official website**.

www.mojosiedlak.com

facebook.com/mojosiedlak
twitter.com/mojosiedlak
instagram.com/mojosiedlak
pinterest.com/mojosiedlak
bookbub.com/authors/monique-joiner-siedlak

More Books by Monique Joiner Siedlak

Practical Magick
Wiccan Basics
Candle Magick
Wiccan Spells
Love Spells
Abundance Spells
Herb Magick
Moon Magick
Creating Your Own Spells
Gypsy Magic
Protection Magick
Celtic Magick
Shamanic Magick

Personal and Self Development
Creative Visualization
Astral Projection for Beginners
Meditation for Beginners
Reiki for Beginners
Manifesting With the Law of Attraction
Stress Management

Time Bound
Healing Animals with Reiki
Being an Empath Today

The Yoga Collective
Yoga for Beginners
Yoga for Stress
Yoga for Back Pain
Yoga for Weight Loss
Yoga for Flexibility
Yoga for Advanced Beginners
Yoga for Fitness
Yoga for Runners
Yoga for Energy
Yoga for Your Sex Life
Yoga To Beat Depression and Anxiety
Yoga for Menstruation
Yoga to Detox Your Body
Yoga to Tone Your Body

A Natural Beautiful You
Creating Your Own Body Butter
Creating Your Own Body Scrub
Creating Your Own Body Spray